**insight text guide**

Scott Hurley

# Hard Times

## Charles Dickens

First published in 2006, reprinted in 2008, 2020.

Insight Publications Pty Ltd
3/350 Charman Road
Cheltenham VIC 3192
Australia
Tel: +61 3 8571 4950
Fax: +61 3 8571 0257
Email: books@insightpublications.com.au

**www.insightpublications.com.au**



National Library of Australia Cataloguing-in-Publication data:
Hurley, Scott.
Charles Dickens' Hard Times: text guide.
For secondary students.
ISBN 9781921088643
1. Dickens, Charles, 1812–1870. Hard Times. I. Title.
823.8

Other ISBNs:
9781922378798 (digital)
9781922378804 (bundle: print + digital)

Cover design by Gisela Beer, based on a concept by The Modern Art Production Group

Printed in Australia by Ligare

# contents

# CHARACTER MAP

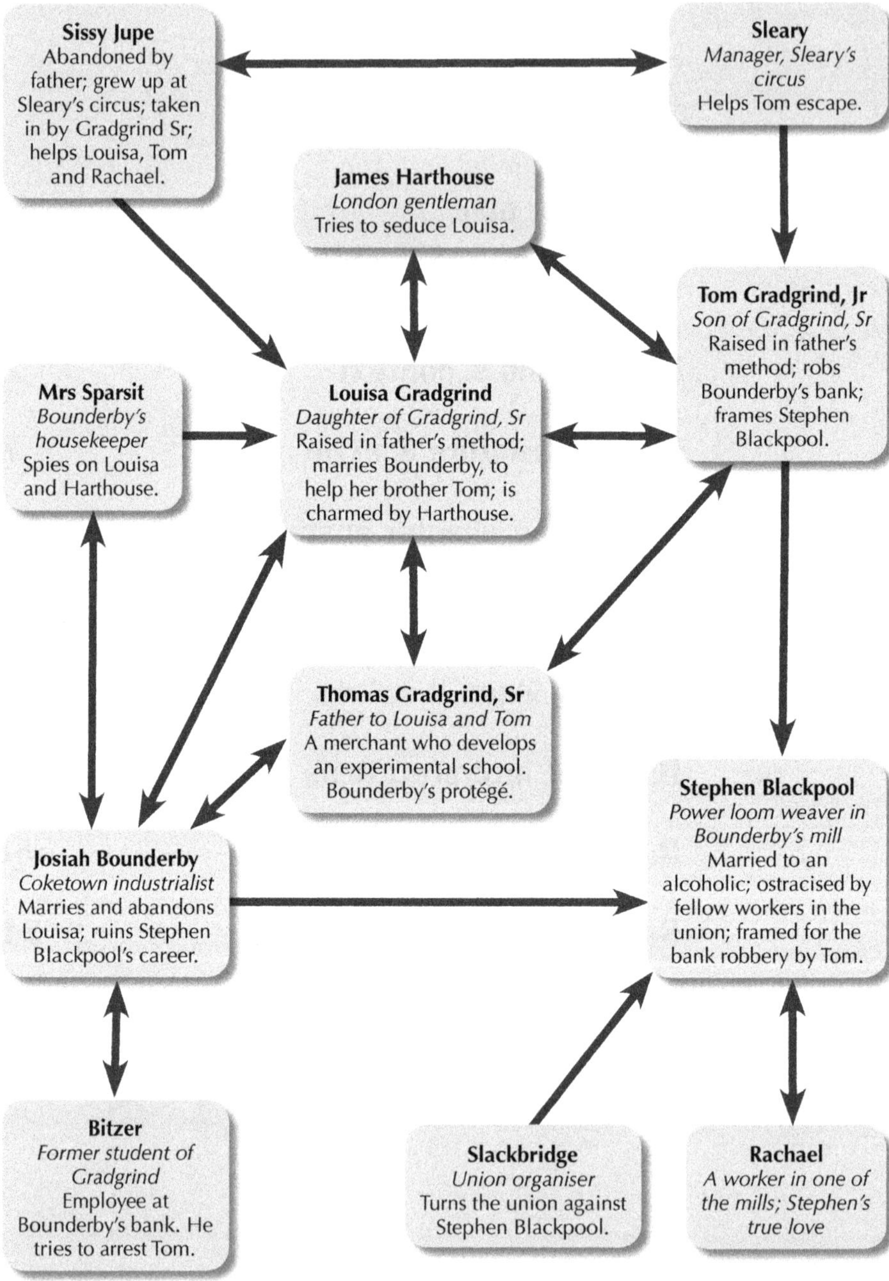

# INTRODUCTION

Written in 1854, *Hard Times* is Charles Dickens' exposé of some of the social inequities created by the industrial boom in early Victorian England. Less an attack on excess than on the oppression of the working classes, it focuses on the quasi-philosophical notions employed by a society, that considers itself highly moral, to excuse inequity and even to justify it. The very model of such rationalisation, Thomas Gradgrind of Coketown, has established a school in which fancy and wonder are abolished in favour of '[f]acts, sir; nothing but Facts!' (p.9). This is an arid world of utilitarianism (see Background & context for further discussion of this concept) and rational political economy[1] where statistics rule and 'facts' are tools to paint a fine picture of an immoral world.

Louisa and Tom, the oldest of Gradgrind's children, are forced to live under this tyranny of fact both at school and at home. *Hard Times* follows them from their lost childhood into a maturity for which neither has been prepared. Tom becomes a 'monster of grovelling sensualities' (p.132), and Louisa is disastrously married to Coketown's most prominent industrialist, the abominable Josiah Bounderby. The novel also tells the stories of others blown by the prevailing winds: Sissy Jupe, abandoned by her father and raised in the Gradgrind household and Stephen Blackpool, one of the working poor in Bounderby's factory. Caught between his restless fellow workers, who have organised themselves into an early form of what we now call a union, and Bounderby, Stephen is demonised by both and hounded out of Coketown. For her part, Sissy quietly begins a revolution of kindness and imagination in the Gradgrind household that will have a recuperative (healing) effect on Louisa and show Gradgrind the error of his philosophy.

---

1 *Rational political economy* refers to an economic model that conceives of people as being 'rational' and 'self-interested' individuals. This model assumes that a person will always act to 'get the best deal' from the information they have. That is, the individual seeks to attain their goals with the least possible cost. Part of the way *Hard Times* works is to make fun of Gradgrind's ridiculous application of this economic principle to all phases of life at the school and in his family.

# BACKGROUND & CONTEXT

## The England of Dickens' time

England was the first industrialised nation of the world, the model on which the Industrial Revolution of the nineteenth century would base itself, for better or worse, in the United States and the countries of continental Europe. Dickens' Coketown is not a thinly disguised Leeds or Sheffield or Manchester, rather it is stand-in for them, an emblematic place containing all that was wrong with these rapidly developing centres of industry. Until early in the nineteenth century they had been relatively small towns, but with the Industrial Revolution, they were transforming, essentially overnight, into polluted, overcrowded cities. In addition, an enormous division of wealth was emerging between the rich, who owned the factories, and the poor, who worked in them.

It was a true revolution. The invention and use of new machinery to speed the process of manufacturing cotton in Manchester, for example, created a need for a cheap workforce. This was supplied by rural areas from all over England, but particularly in the north where there had been high birth rates and diminishing opportunities for years. In three decades (between 1810 and 1841) the population of Leeds tripled; in Manchester it went from 95,000 to 310,000. Yet other inventions, like the power loom[2] (Stephen Blackpool is a power loom operator) actually reduced the need for labour, creating enough unemployment to give the mill owners power to set the conditions for work. There were no regulations; wages were low and hours were exceedingly long. The 15-hour shifts Dickens describes are not an exaggeration, and they were worked by children too. In fact, in some of the mills, the great majority of workers were under 18. Absent too were any regulations concerning what we now call industrial health and safety. The new machines could be extremely dangerous. You can imagine the terrible loss of life and limb from the deadly dance

2 A machine for weaving yarn into thread that was powered by an engine.

between raw machinery and the workers meant to operate it. They were overworked, underfed, untrained, perhaps fresh from a rural existence and completely alien to the factory environment, perhaps ten years old, perhaps younger.

Outside work, things were scarcely better. Living conditions for the working poor became more squalid, dangerous and unhealthy the more people came flooding in for jobs. No city can properly accommodate such an increase of population in so short a time, but then no one seems really to have tried. The growing class of manufacturers and professional and merchant trades associated with manufacturing (sometimes referred to as the *bourgeoisie*) kept themselves in fashionable precincts well apart from the slums. They enjoyed the increasing benefits and services possible only in the new modern economy, while the working classes languished in conditions of a depravity never witnessed before. The slums were magnets for diseases of the day: smallpox, tuberculosis, cholera, typhoid and syphilis. Crime and prostitution were rampant and families were often divided, leaving children to make their own way. Mortality rates reached levels unheard of since the time of the Black Death.[3] In 1841, in the industrial cities of the north, life expectancy at birth was well under thirty![4] This is a world of contrasts. The style of living pursued by the manufacturers and other new capitalists was something that few outside the aristocracy could even have dreamed about in previous centuries; yet the 'hands' could barely survive on the wages paid for unspeakable hours. The civic pride of these new capitalists, fed by the competition between the great industrial cities themselves, produced unprecedented donations to cultural institutions. Despite this new wealth, the workers had to survive in living conditions that can only be described as medieval. The rivers were choked with effluent and, hovering over all the glittering palaces and groomed neighbourhoods were the clouds of smoke belching from chimneys and the poisonous, unseen gases produced by manufacturing.

3 The Black Death was a great epidemic of bubonic plague that occurred in fourteenth-century Europe. It killed between a third and two-thirds of the population of Europe.

4 See Brewer, John 2006, 'City Lights', *The New York Review of Books*, vol. 53, no. 8.

Eventually efforts were organised to make life a bit better for workers. The 1830s saw the introduction of several reform bills; work by children under nine years of age was prohibited, for example, and the number of hours that children older than that could work was regulated. Yet some of the reforms created worse conditions, like the institution of the workhouses, which Dickens wrote about in a number of his other stories. The poor, many of whom were itinerant – going from place to place to find seasonal work – were forced to live in these workhouses with their families, confined and little more than slaves. The Chartist Movement of the 1840s, which focused primarily on the requirements for members of parliament and the procedures by which they were elected, was the first great working-class movement in England. It failed, but not before alerting the country to the plight of workers, and alarming it with riots and social upheaval. Learning from this experience, workers organised themselves and created labour unions. Unions were illegal when *Hard Times* was written, but they became legal in 1864 and slowly created better conditions for workers.

## Some of Dickens' philosophical targets

The climate of reform and political economy found in *Hard Times* is a reflection of some of the philosophical discussion of Dickens' day, as influenced by the thinkers of a generation or two before it. In the novel Thomas Gradgrind practises a utilitarianism that seems to be a sort of mixture of ideas to be found in the principles of theorists like Adam Smith, Thomas Malthus, Jeremy Bentham and John Stuart Mill.

In the late 1700s, Smith (1723–1790) proposed that self-seeking in individuals, far from being a liability to an economy, was like an 'invisible hand' guiding it to advancement. He propounded a laissez-faire capitalism (French for 'leave alone'), in which the drive for self-betterment by competitors is left to sort itself out, without governmental interference, to the betterment of the entire economy. Though Smith was writing even before the advent of the Industrial Revolution this is a proposition very much with us today (even if the full measure of his ideas is not always invoked).

Malthus (1766–1834), though also an economist, remains best known for his writings on the dangers of overpopulation. Proposing that population will always run slightly ahead of a society's ability to cope with it, Malthus questioned the idea that a nation's population was an indication of its prosperity; he believed that poverty was inescapable, and that charity and laws intended to relieve the plight of the poor increased population, and therefore decreased the overall health of the society. Thus, he was opposed to providing charity, or welfare 'safety nets', for the poor in society. Though his conclusions were callous, his ideas were very influential.

Jeremy Bentham (1748–1832), a follower of Adam Smith, and John Stuart Mill (1806–1873) developed utilitarianism as a philosophy. They developed the idea that legislation should be directed towards a single aim – 'the greatest happiness of the greatest number'. *Utility* is the property of producing good or happiness, or preventing pain or unhappiness. In other words, utilitarianism proposes that acts should be evaluated in terms of their results or consequences, rather than whether they agree with a moral rule. Thus an *action* is judged to be 'right' or 'wrong' based on its ability to produce happiness or the opposite of happiness. Previous philosophical positions tended to make *a priori* judgements[5] of the 'rightness' of an action, based on an existing moral code. We see this conflict at play in the novel in Book 1, Chapter 9, when M'Choakumchild keeps firing questions biased towards a utilitarian world view ('the greatest happiness of the greatest number') and Sissy keeps responding to them out of a moral code based on empathy and charity. The name of the chapter ('Sissy's Progress') is an allusion to John Bunyan's *The Pilgrim's Progress*, an allegorical treatment of Christian morality and one of the most famous works in English literature. Throughout *Hard Times*,

---

5 *A priori* is Latin for 'from first principles'. In this context, it refers to judgements that people make based on a presumption, such as what they've been taught or believe, rather than from a proper examination of the issue.

Dickens sets Gradgrind's utilitarianism in direct opposition to traditional Christian codes of moral behaviour.

The teaching philosophy of Gradgrind, then, incorporates the self-interest to be found in Smith, the dismissal of charity to be found in Malthus and the pursuit of utility to be found in Bentham. To support his ideas Bentham maintained that human pleasure and pain could literally be calculated, mathematically, in a bizarre formula he called a 'felicific calculus'. In this he seems quite a bit like Gradgrind, 'with his little mean excise-rod' (p.216), working out *his* calculations for human happiness. Yet I think it is a mistake to think Dickens had a single person in mind as his target. Rather, he was attacking what he saw as a spirit of the time, materialistic and mechanical, that was responsible for dehumanising much of the society in the interest of progressing it. Like his friend Thomas Carlyle, to whom *Hard Times* is dedicated, Dickens decried utilitarianism's tendency to dismiss morality in favour of cold statistics and sterile reasoning.

# GENRE, STRUCTURE & STYLE

*Hard Times* is a novel very much in keeping with its period – the Victorian era. This is hardly a surprise, considering that Dickens is its greatest proponent. (Other noteworthy English novelists of the time, Trollope, Thackeray, Eliot and Collins, are not only read considerably less today than Dickens, they also seem more remote from our image, right or wrong, of the Victorians.)

## Publication as a serial (week by week)

Dickens was extraordinarily popular in his day, and he employed some far-sighted techniques to get the most financial benefit out of this popularity. Like many of his other works, *Hard Times* first came out in instalments in Dickens' own magazine *Household Words*.[6] This reality has an undeniable influence on the way the novel is written. Like all of Dickens' long works, it has a broad scope, following a variety of characters over long periods of time, sometimes over entire lives. The chapters of *Hard Times* are of a length to hold the interest of his magazine's readers (for one instalment), and they move between characters at a pace intended to get readers involved with the 'stories' of its numerous characters.[7] Think of modern-day soap operas, and you get the picture. This is not intended as an insult; no author ever knew his readership better than Dickens, and he worked hard to keep them reading his works. Perhaps the greatest reason for this, beyond matters financial, is that Dickens was a true reformer. Most of his novels had strong didactic elements, none more so than *Hard Times*. The greater the readership, the further his message was broadcast.

6 Circulation increased greatly in the issues carrying instalments of the novel. After it had all appeared in *Household Words, Hard Times* was then sold to a publisher, to begin a new life as a book.

7 Dickens only divided *Hard Times* into its three titled books ('Sowing', 'Reaping' and 'Garnering') for publication of the novel as a book after its run in *Household Words*. This was also when he gave names to the chapters.

## *Hard Times* has a strong message

*Hard Times* differs from Dickens' other novels in its brevity. Perhaps the shortest of them all, it is not even half the length of masterpieces like *Bleak House* or *David Copperfield*. Likewise it has many fewer characters than his more ambitious books. Though there are strong 'messages' in other works by the author, *Hard Times* differs from *Bleak House, David Copperfield* or *Great Expectations* (at least for this reader) in its privileging of message over character. What one remembers in *Hard Times* is Dickens rage at the inequity rampant in the Coketowns of England. From this rage blossoms the work's finest writing – it is not to be found in the characters of *Hard Times* or in its rather contrived situations. There are exceptions: Josiah Bounderby is certainly memorable, but only because he is such a caricature. The characters whom we are meant to feel the most sympathy for – Louisa, Stephen, Rachael, even Tom – never find lives of their own outside the didactic labours their author puts them to. One feels that these characters were created first to make a point, and that their actions are choreographed solely for this purpose.

## *Hard Times* as melodrama

Dickens also makes his point through the reader's emotional response to the characters' situations. Dickens is known for being melodramatic; there is no escaping it. Throughout his works are famous set pieces, such as the death of Little Nell in *The Old Curiosity Shop*, for example, which are downright unscrupulous in their manipulation of our emotional response. There are scenes of such overcooked pathos[8] that we now snicker about them, almost as a reflex, much in the way we might if someone says something grossly, embarrassingly inappropriate. Victorian readers ate this bathetic[9] fare with a spoon, and it played no small part in Dickens' popularity.

---

8 *Pathos* refers to the feelings of sympathetic sadness inspired by a text or event.

9 *Bathetic* describes the sudden shift from the beautiful or profound to the silly and ridiculous.

Behind the melodrama is, of course, a lesson; Dickens' sympathies are always with the powerless, he encourages the powerful to corrective action – if Scrooge will reform himself, Tiny Tim will not have to die.[10] But in *Hard Times* the melodrama falls pretty flat (think of Stephen and Rachael's impossible love and their vows to be together after death, of Louisa's 'suffering the wreck of her life on the rock' (p.216) because of Harthouse's proposal). It is hard to identify emotionally with a pawn; they are moved by the chess-player along their plodding course, sacrificed when necessary, rarely missed. A hundred and sixty years on, we can almost hear Dickens labouring to instil some pathos into the pawns that are the characters of *Hard Times*. Unfortunately, his attempts are all in vain, and the harder he labours, the more we snicker.

## Richness of imagination and expression

If Dickens is known for his melodrama, he is also known for his exuberance. There is a richness of expression and a fertility of imagination one can find in few other writers. Writing must have been a joy for Dickens. He seems to relish getting things just right in his descriptions of his characters, a generous flow of detail that makes them so memorable. In *Hard Times*, this exuberance is expressed most obviously in his writing about Coketown. He describes its ever-present mantle of smoke, its 'melancholy-mad elephants' of machinery (p.71), its oppressors, its victims, its reformers. Coketown is a kind of trap, wholly of the making of modern social conditions: capitalism, industry, economic rationalism and utilitarianism. It is an embodiment of what is wrong with the times as Dickens sees it.

---

10 This refers to characters in Dickens' *A Christmas Carol*.

## Dickens' voice

Dickens was very passionate about his critique of what he saw as being wrong with the way the world was heading. His writing on these issues rises to a level not present elsewhere in the novel. Outside of first-person narratives, we are not accustomed to the voice Dickens employs here in contemporary fiction; it is intrusive, opinionated and full of its own importance. His contemporary, the great French novelist Gustave Flaubert, is famous for declaring that the author of a novel should disappear into the work. This was not the method for Dickens; he wants to be our guide, to lead our opinions, to inform us of important aspects to his story, to rail against certain characters and defend others. It can sometimes be a bit too much: he might underscore a moral point already made obvious in the course of the novel's action or dialogue or he might state a conclusion that we should really have been left to determine ourselves. But this too is a result of his exuberance, of his need to right wrongs. Regarding the terrible world he saw in industrial, Victorian England, Dickens does not leave our outrage to chance.

# CHAPTER-BY-CHAPTER ANALYSIS

## 'Book the First: Sowing'

## Chapters 1–3: 'The One Thing Needful'; 'Murdering the Innocents'; 'A Loophole' (pp.9–20)

**Summary:** *Thomas Gradgrind, his school and his philosophy of education are introduced.*

*Hard Times* begins in the school Thomas Gradgrind, an industrialist, has founded to educate some of the children of Coketown. Its philosophy can be summed up in his instructions to M'Choakumchild, the schoolmaster: 'You can only form the minds of reasoning animals upon Facts: nothing else will ever be of any service to them' (p.9). The first chapter's title comes from the Bible, Luke 10:42, where Jesus instructs an overworked Martha to attend to the 'one thing needful' – following God. Dickens is telling us that Gradgind is making a god of facts.

In class, Sissy Jupe is unable to define a horse to Gradgrind's liking (she has been around horses all her life and so would know more about them than anyone in the room). Bitzer's 'factual' definition, no more than a zoological profile, pleases Gradgrind enormously. The third adult in this classroom, a governmental inspector of some kind, takes up the cause. It is not enough to privilege 'facts' in education; imagination, or 'fancy' of any kind is strictly forbidden. The second chapter title's biblical allusion is less subtle than that of the first: Gradgrind's students are the 'innocents', and their individuality will be 'murdered' in the pursuit of cold facts.

***Q*** Why has Dickens written the government official into this scene?

As he walks home from school, Gradgrind is mortified to discover his two oldest children trying to see into Sleary's horse-circus. This is precisely the kind of entertainment – coarse, imaginative and exciting – they, who have had no songs, stories or nursery rhymes, who have not been allowed to exercise their imaginations in any way, are to avoid at all costs.

## Chapters 4–6: 'Mr Bounderby'; 'The Key-note'; 'Sleary's Horsemanship' (pp.20–46)

**Summary:** *We meet Josiah Bounderby, are introduced to Coketown and visit Sleary's circus.*

Josiah Bounderby, a boastful bully, awaits his friend Gradgrind at the latter's house, called, coldly enough, Stone Lodge. He is relating invented stories of his childhood poverty and abuse to the peevish and stupid Mrs Gradgrind when Gradgrind announces what he has caught his children doing. Mrs Gradgrind reacts strongly, but not because she particularly shares her husband's philosophy. Weak and self-centred, she hates controversy and would rather not hear from her children at all. Bounderby and Gradgrind conclude that it is Sissy Jupe's presence at the school that has led Tom and Louisa astray. They head off to Coketown to tell Sissy's father that she may no longer attend – but not before Bounderby purloins (steals) a kiss from Louisa, more than 30 years his junior.

Dickens is at his best in the kind of descriptive writing found in Chapter 5. Coketown is, paradoxically, both sterile and filthy. Dedicated to manufacturing, it is forever palled in smoke and blackened by soot, and for the same reason it is devoid of anything of cultural value. A no-nonsense town, 'factual' in the Gradgrind sense, Coketown's labourers are over-worked, underfed, oppressed by the dictates of Victorian industrialisation. They long for 'physical relief ... good humour and good spirits' (p.30), but find only monotonous work. Yet their employers, men like Gradgrind and Bounderby, see them as selfish and lazy. Dickens' use of animal imagery ('serpents of smoke', elephant-like machines, p.27) is purposeful. It characterises Coketown as a dehumanised, unnatural place.

Chapter 6 is most notable for its contrasts. Their outlandish costumes, their colourful occupations and their rootlessness make the performers of Sleary's circus the very antitheses (opposites) of Gradgrind and Bounderby. Their expressions practically constitute a foreign language, but more importantly, they are kind-hearted people, a 'family' dedicated to looking after each other – qualities definitely contrasting to those of the gentlemen from Coketown. The horseman, Childers, tells Gradgrind that Sissy's father has abandoned her and the circus, because it broke his heart for Sissy to see him fail. Gradgrind makes an offer – against Bounderby's advice – for Sissy to join his household, under the condition that she leave Sleary's circus forever.

***Q*** Does this offer represent a spark of kindness in Gradgrind, or does he see it as an opportunity to test his educational method?

## Chapters 7–10: 'Mrs Sparsit'; 'Never Wonder'; 'Sissy's Progress' (pp.46–65)

**Summary:** *We meet Mrs Sparsit and glimpse into the lives of Tom and Louisa; Sissy discusses her father.*

Dickens' description of Mrs Sparsit's pedigree is delicious. Dickens uses her to send up England's minor aristocracy, which is characterised as gluttonous and wasteful, and displaying unspeakable pride in its noble lineage, even when the family fortune has long ago been gambled or drunk away. Mrs Sparsit keeps house for him, but the real service she provides for Bounderby lies elsewhere. His hypocritical deference to her station is merely a way to revalidate his delusional idea of himself as the 'self-made man'. Having decided that Sissy will work in his household, Gradgrind comes, with Louisa, to collect her from Bounderby's house where she has stayed since leaving Sleary's circus. We should note Louisa's basic indifference to poor Sissy's plight – signs of an emotional flatness created by her upbringing.

Chapter 8's title – 'Never Wonder' – comes from the words Gradgrind the elder used to reprimand Louisa for once beginning a sentence 'I wonder …'. This leads on to a description of Coketown's eighteen different denominations (influential groups in the town): though they all talk about 'improving' the workers of the city, they can only agree upon this single injunction – *never wonder*. The following conversation between Louisa and young Tom reveals that curiosity has not quite been excised from

Louisa, yet she sees her life as dull and essentially meaningless, devoid of all the things – stories, art, music, imagination, in a word, 'wonder' – she suspects go to making it worth living. Tom, bitter and scheming, intends to use the opportunity to join Bounderby's office to enact revenge against his sterile upbringing. He knows that Bounderby is enamoured of Louisa and intends to use that to his advantage. A distinction between the children is already established: where Louisa's first thoughts are to making Tom's life easier, however she can, Tom's are to using his sister to his own advantage.

Louisa and Sissy discuss the latter's difficulty getting anything right at the school. Her answers are of course all derived from the basic tenets of Christian morality. (She even mistakes, 'To do unto others as I would that they should do unto me', as the first principle of political economy, p.59.) That her answers are deemed hopelessly wrong indicts the school's philosophy rather than Sissy. The story of her father, of the clown who cried when he couldn't make anyone laugh, etc., is almost too sentimental. Yet Victorians loved this kind of thing, and Dickens was the master of it. More important is Sissy's faith in her father and her hope that he will return to her.

## Chapters 10–13: 'Stephen Blackpool'; 'No Way Out'; 'The Old Woman'; 'Rachael' (pp.65–90)

**Summary:** *A new group of characters, and their stories, is introduced.*

Chapter 10 follows the movements of Stephen Blackpool, one of the labourers or 'hands' of Coketown. He meets with Rachael after a long workday, and their conversation reveals that they love each other, but are kept apart by something. That something is Stephen's alcoholic wife, whom he finds in his small room after one of her long absences. In his conversation with Bounderby, Stephen reveals that he has put up with his wayward wife for 19 years and is desperate for some way out of the marriage. Bounderby explains that there is no recourse for him; divorce requires an Act of Parliament, a thing completely beyond Stephen's means. Bounderby can't resist a pompous lecture on the sanctity of marriage and on Stephen's taking his wife for better or worse – he will show his hypocrisy later in the book when he simply declares his marriage to Louisa over. Afterwards, Stephen meets an old woman who walks many miles and rides the cheap train just to gaze at Bounderby's house and his factory. She will be revealed, towards the novel's end, to be his mother, a simple, strange woman, overwhelmed by her hypocrite son's great rise in the world.

Stephen returns to work, dreading the hour when he will have to go home and meet his estranged wife. He thinks about Rachael and all the years of happiness they've lost because of his marriage. Later, despondent and ruminating on death, he returns to find Rachael tending to his wife, who is delirious with drink and a danger to herself. The sight of a bottle of poison has put dark thoughts into Stephen's head. In a fitful sleep, he dreams of his own hanging, the foreseeable consequence if he follows his impulse to kill her. But his wife nearly drinks the poison herself as Rachael sleeps; Rachael wakes up just in time to prevent it. She is a ministering angel, for both husband and wife.

## Chapters 14–16: 'The Great Manufacturer'; 'Father and Daughter'; 'Husband and Wife' (pp.90–108)

**Summary:** *A few years later, Tom is working at Bounderby's bank and Louisa has grown into a young woman; Louisa accepts Bounderby's proposal of marriage and they marry.*

### Key chapters: 14 & 15

'The Great Manufacturer' of Chapter 14 is time, and Dickens has some fine writing here about how it creates new people out of the old in its 'factory'. Gradgrind has become MP for Coketown. Sissy, has never improved at the school and so is ending her studies. Tom is with Bounderby, and Louisa is still staring at the ashes of the fire, only now she has grown into a 'young woman'. It is time for something to happen in her life. Young Tom comes for a rare visit, and implies that Bounderby wants to marry Louisa. He also lets her know that the marriage would be beneficial to his career. When Gradgrind tells Louisa that Bounderby has asked to marry her, she does not know how to react. Her upbringing has not prepared her for matters of love. When she asks her father's advice, predictably, he spouts statistics regarding marriages in England and Wales.

### Key point

In this crucial moment in Gradgrind and Louisa's relationship he fails her completely, not even suspecting what the doubts and fears and hopes of this young woman could be. When she points out to him that he has never let her be a child (and so, by implication, is not prepared to make an adult decision), he takes it as a great compliment.

Louisa has never been taught to value anything in life except facts and statistics, so she is incapable of making a decision of the heart. Her 'what does it matter?' indicates that she sees her life merely as a series of events, no single one more important than another one. What does it matter, then, who her husband is to be?

The biggest problem for Bounderby, now that Louisa has accepted him is what to do with Mrs Sparsit, who cannot stay on to run his household. He finds her surprisingly easy to manage, but she takes on an unshakeable attitude of pity for Bounderby in his choice of bride. Louisa remains indifferent as the preparations take place and the wedding day comes. The only one who seems truly happy about the match is Tom.

## 'Book the Second: Reaping'

## Chapters 1–3: 'Effects in the Bank'; 'Mr James Harthouse'; 'The Whelp' (pp.111–36)

**Summary:** *Mrs Sparsit in her new lodgings at the bank; the introduction of Mr Harthouse; Harthouse works on Tom to find out more about Louisa.*

Moved from Bounderby's house, Mrs Sparsit is kept abreast of the gossip in the bank (though she pretends to be above such things) by her 'light-porter', Bitzer, Sissy's former tormenter. Their talk has a nasty edge to it, beyond their disparagements of the 'hands' of Coketown (notice how their sentiments are cut from the same cloth as those of Bounderby, even though they themselves are only servants). Bitzer is a climber, looking for advancement; Mrs Sparsit is looking for an opportunity to work her way back into the comfort of Bounderby's home. To the bank comes James Harthouse, who has everything, sees value in nothing, and has decided to 'go in for' Gradgrind's statistical method on a whim. A meeting with Bounderby almost changes his mind, but fascination for the beautiful, enigmatic Louisa makes him decide to stay on, if only to try to understand her. He is honest with her about his total lack of conviction in anything; his 'any set of ideas will do just as much good as any other set' (p.129), sounds suspiciously like her 'what does it matter?' from Book 1, Chapter 15. We will see that there are indeed many similarities between Gradgrind's utilitarianism and Harthouse's nihilism.[11] In Chapter 3, Dickens gives us a full measure of Tom's character, showing how Harthouse's name for him ('the whelp', a derogatory name for a youth) is just right. In the course of a drink and a smoke (is there something stronger than tobacco in those cigars?), Tom reveals that Louisa is unhappy in her marriage and naïve about the real workings of the world – in other words, that she is ripe to be exploited by someone like Harthouse.

## Chapters 4–6: 'Men and Brothers'; 'Men and Masters'; 'Fading Away' (pp.136–62)

**Summary:** *Stephen Blackpool is told off and excluded by the union at Bounderby's factory; he is dismissed by Bounderby and visited by Louisa and Tom before leaving Coketown.*

### Key chapter: 5

Stephen has been the only one of the workers in Bounderby's factory not to sign on to agitate for new regulations in this early form of unionist activity. It is never stated what his objections are, even by Stephen. Something seems missing here. In the next chapter, we will learn that he is honour-bound by a promise, but we have not heard what it is. Notice how unfavourably Dickens regards the whole proceedings

11 *Nihilism* means not believing in anything.

– the speaker Slackbridge is portrayed as a manipulative rabblerouser, and it is decided that Stephen will be ostracised (cut off) from the only companions he has ever known. Calling him to his house, Bounderby wants to know why Stephen has not gone along with his union but ends up provoking Stephen into defending his co-workers, despite their attitude towards him. In a nutshell, Stephen describes the 'muddle' that is Victorian labour relations, and how it will never be solved by demonising the workers, or showing force against them, or arresting their leaders. These are pretty clearly the positions of Dickens himself, put into the language of Stephen Blackpool.

***Q*** Why is it ironic that Bounderby fires Stephen for this response?

The old woman, called Mrs Pegler, is again watching Bounderby's house, this time in Rachael's company, when Stephen leaves. Notice how polite Stephen is, even after receiving such a blow from Bounderby. Back at his room, they are visited by Louisa. Uncharacteristically moved by Stephen's dignified performance, she has come to offer him some money. Tom has an idea of his own. In private, he contrives to get Blackpool to hang around the bank for an hour or so each night until he leaves Coketown.

## Chapters 7–9: 'Gunpowder'; 'Explosion'; 'Hearing the Last of It' (pp.162–94)

**Summary:** *Harthouse begins to work his way into Louisa's good favour; Stephen Blackpool is suspected of a robbery at the bank; Louisa is summoned home to her dying mother.*

Her recent charity soon forgotten, Louisa begins to be impressed by Harthouse's nihilism. She sees how his refusal to believe that anything matters agrees perfectly with the philosophy of life that her upbringing has given her.

### Key point

Indeed, Harthouse is merely another of the 'never wonder' crowd. Different from Louisa's father in almost every respect, Harthouse's philosophy nevertheless produces precisely the same results.

Determined to conquer Louisa sexually, Harthouse attacks her weakest flank: her affection for Tom. He gains her confidence about Tom's gambling debts that she has been bankrolling. After the robbery Mrs Sparsit takes the opportunity to insinuate herself back into Bounderby's household, and she immediately begins to undermine Louisa's standing. Louisa, suspecting Tom of committing the robbery, tries to get him to make a confession late at night, to no avail. His refusal even to talk to her implies that he is past redemption.

Called back to Stone Lodge, Louisa reflects on why she has been there so seldom since her marriage. The fact is that there are no happy memories for her there, just the 'drying up of every spring and fountain in her young heart as it gushed out' (p.192). Mrs Gradgrind's death is no more edifying than her life, though, curiously, she senses that there is some kind of knowledge to be had that is not covered in all the '-ologies' Gradgrind has taught in his school. Sleary completes this idea later in the novel when he talks about the importance of love (Book 3, Chapter 8).

## Chapters 10–12: 'Mrs Sparsit's Staircase'; 'Lower and Lower'; 'Down' (pp.195–212)

**Summary:** *Mrs Sparsit keeps her eye on Louisa and Harthouse, and then follows them to a secret meeting; Louisa returns to Stone Lodge seeking her father's help.*

Mrs Sparsit, desiring to overthrow Louisa from the place she once occupied, keeps a constant watch on Louisa and Harthouse, certain that they are descending a 'staircase' into disgrace. In a conversation she observes, but does not overhear, Harthouse tries to convince Louisa that Blackpool is guilty of the robbery at the bank, just as Bounderby asserts. It is an attempt to drag her down a different staircase, into his own debased ideas about human beings. Louisa finds Harthouse's philosophy tempting: 'what does it matter' is easier on the conscience than the alternative, which is to see the good in people like Blackpool, and to work to preserve that good against men like Bounderby and Harthouse.

In the next chapter, Mrs Sparsit thinks she is about to catch Harthouse and Louisa in an adulterous act that will destroy Louisa's reputation. She sees them together and overhears Harthouse's declaration of desire for Louisa, and their arrangement to meet each other that night. She follows Louisa through a forest during a violent rainstorm, but loses her at a railway station.

### Key chapter: 12

Rather than meet Harthouse for their rendezvous, Louisa returns home, having nowhere else to go. She bluntly tells her father her feelings about his destruction of her childhood with his teaching method, about how it has made her unprepared for adulthood. She tells him that she has never loved Bounderby, and suggests that he knew it and did nothing to stop her from marrying him. It is a juicy, melodramatic scene. The chapter finishes with Louisa telling her father about her plight with Harthouse. Harthouse's declaration of love for Louisa and her disappearing from the house have the hallmarks of an enormous scandal. She demands that her father find a meaningful way to help her, without any of his philosophical claptrap, to compensate her for the damage he has done.

## 'Book the Third: Garnering'

## Chapters 1–3: 'Another Thing Needful'; 'Very Ridiculous'; 'Very Decided' (pp.215–38)

**Summary:** *The ramifications of Louisa's aborted meeting with Harthouse and her return to Stone Lodge.*

There are reconciliations and separations in these chapters, all to Louisa's good. Her father admits that his educational system has been a disaster to her. At a loss as to how to help her out of her difficulty, he pledges to try. Louisa's reconciliation with Sissy is of more practical value. (It was her expression of pity back in Book 1, Chapter 15, that had hardened Louisa towards her.)

Sissy has been a transformative power at Stone Lodge, giving the love and comfort to the younger children that was kept from Louisa and Tom.

She takes it upon herself to dismiss James Harthouse from the scene, going alone to his hotel to tell him he cannot see Louisa again, and that he should leave Coketown immediately. The poseur is no match for the 'stroller's daughter', and indeed does slink away.

There is an interesting parallel between Gradgrind and Harthouse in these two chapters. Both men, known for being able to talk the ears off a cornstalk in their different endeavours, find themselves at a loss for words when confronted with the truth of their failures. Both mutter vague protests about not really intending any harm, though their harm has been incalculable.

No such self-consciousness is visited upon Bounderby. In the third chapter, he confronts Gradgrind with Mrs Sparsit's testimony that Louisa has been canoodling with Harthouse. The testimony is proven false to his face but this makes not the slightest difference to him. Instead, he makes an impossible ultimatum that severs his relations with both Louisa and Gradgrind, ending the marriage. Dickens takes pains to remind us of Bounderby's previous, hypocritical position on the sanctity of marriage when Stephen Blackpool came to him for help in his own affairs (Book 1, Chapter 11).

## Chapters 4–6: 'Lost'; 'Found'; 'The Starlight' (pp.238–65)

**Summary:** *Bounderby offers a reward for the capture of Stephen Blackpool and all await his return.*

To get the case moving, Bounderby offers a £20 reward. Slackbridge uses the notice to further demonise Stephen to the union, convicting him without trial, as Bounderby has done. Rachael promises to send a letter that will get Stephen to return. Her visit to Louisa gets Sissy involved in trying to clear Stephen's name. Unspoken between Sissy and Louisa is the suspicion that Tom is behind the robbery. All await Stephen's return, but he doesn't appear. In the meantime, Mrs Pegler, whom Bounderby wants to question about her role in the matter, is roughly brought to his house by Mrs Sparsit, acting on her own initiative. Before a full house, including Mr Gradgrind, it is revealed that Mrs Pegler is Bounderby's mother, and that far from abusing him as a child, she had been a model mother. It turns out that Bounderby has concocted his story of neglect out of nothing.

On the following Sunday, while walking in the country to refresh their spirits, Sissy and Rachael discover that Stephen has fallen down an abandoned mine shaft, while on his way back to Coketown to clear his name. A frenetic rescue ensues and Stephen, finally brought out, delivers a last prolonged speech before dying. He recounts that he had been on his way to be 'unjust' to Louisa, as he thought she and her brother had been to him, but that he realised that we must 'bear and forbear'. He laments that so many men have died in the pits when they were operating and that they are still dying in them after they have been abandoned. He asks Gradgrind to clear his name after his death, hinting that young Tom had something to do with the robbery of the bank.

### Key point

Stephen is wrongly accused, tried without a chance to defend himself and finally dies because of the realities of modern life in Coketown. It is significant that the mine shaft causes his death – it is the modern world that has destroyed him. He slips away, following the star of the 'Redeemer' – a Christ-figure sacrificed to the sins of modernity.

## Chapters 7–9: 'Whelp-hunting'; 'Philosophical'; 'Final' (pp.265–88)

**Summary:** *Tom runs to Sleary's circus and gets out of the country; the novel closes with some words about the characters' futures.*

Having sent Tom to Sleary's circus on the night of Stephen's death, Sissy leads Gradgrind and Louisa there, where she also has a happy reunion with her one-time 'family'. Sleary agrees to help Gradgrind get Tom to Liverpool and thus out of the country. Confronting his son a last time before this departure, Gradgrind receives only hard words from Tom, reminding Gradgrind of what he himself had taught – that it was a 'law' that a certain number of people placed in positions of trust will behave dishonestly. Gradgrind gets to witness the disastrous results of his method on another of his children. Tom will not reconcile with Louisa, still blaming her for his troubles. Before the party can head for Liverpool, Bitzer arrives, intending to bring Tom back to justice, and will not be swayed from this. He too has been taught well in Gradgrind's method, and to the others' appeals to loyalty, he merely quotes Gradgrind himself on the dictates of self-interest. Sleary distracts Bitzer while Tom gets away and Sleary returns the next morning to inform the party of Tom's escape. Privately, he tells Gradgrind of his belief that Sissy's father had died the previous year.

## Key point

Sleary takes the opportunity to put words to a lesson Gradgrind has had to learn the hard way – that love is a greater force in the world than self-interest.

In a virtuoso final chapter, Dickens dismisses his cast with images of what will become of them. Mrs Sparsit is packed off to Lady Scadgers, but not before showing her utter contempt for Bounderby. Bounderby himself dies of a fit five years later and his will is fought over by scavengers for years after that. Gradgrind tries to employ his newfound empathy in Parliament and is ridiculed by his fellow members. Rachael works at her labours and does what she can for Stephen's widow. Sissy has a big family, but Louisa doesn't have one. Instead, she dedicates herself to ensuring that other children get the childhood she never had.

# CHARACTERS & RELATIONSHIPS

## Louisa Gradgrind

**Key quotes**

'I have been tired a long time .... I don't know of what – of everything I think.' (p.20)

'Utterly indifferent, perfectly self-reliant, never at a loss, and yet never at her ease ...' (p.127)

'What I have learned has left me doubting, misbelieving, despising, regretting, what I have not learned; and my dismal resource has been to think that life would soon go by ...' (p.210)

Louisa is the great prisoner of *Hard Times*. Her life in the novel is mostly spent captive to one character or another. It begins when she and her brother Tom are imprisoned by their father's teaching method, which extends beyond the schoolroom to their home at Stone Lodge. Louisa spends most of her time staring at the ashes of the fire, reflecting on the pointlessness of life. Her only consolation is Tom. Later, after he has gone, she takes her first opportunity to escape Stone Lodge: the disastrous decision to accept Bounderby as her husband. This begins her second captivity, as Loo Bounderby, married to Coketown's worst citizen, staring at the falling leaves instead of the fire. That her decision to marry was made partly to protect Tom rebounds against her when her ungrateful brother starts making more demands. Along comes James Harthouse, playing the serpent to her Eve. He seduces her less with his good looks and refinement than with his empty philosophy.

If there is one thing Louisa has come to believe during the course of her unfortunate life, it is that 'nothing matters'. There is a very great difference between Louisa's nihilism, born out of her constricted circumstances, and Harthouse's fashionable apathy. Louisa has never had any choice in life, and has been exposed to nothing but Gradgrind's soul-killing education. Still, Louisa sees Harthouse as a kindred spirit, and more importantly, in his pose that everything is 'hollow and worthless', she finds a 'relief and justification' (p.163) for the very nihilism she has embraced. This attitude has lately been challenged by her feelings of pity for Stephen Blackpool.

**Key point**

In the way that damaged people often find solace in the very beliefs or substances that are destroying them, Louisa finds confirmation of her philosophy in Harthouse. And so she nearly allows herself to move from captivity to Bounderby to captivity to Harthouse, only waking up to the reality of her life when Harthouse's seduction pushes forward to a different kind of fulfilment.

We should remember that in early Victorian England Louisa simply has nowhere else to go but back to her father's house, yet it is ironic that she returns to the scene of her initial captivity in order to be freed from her new captor, Bounderby, and her would-be captor, Harthouse. If Louisa were a real person we would say that she is having a nervous breakdown. She is, of course, a character in a novel by Dickens, and so, at a time when a real person would be incoherent, Louisa makes a clear, eloquent and intellectually vigorous speech (condemning Gradgrind's parenting).

Is it believable that a woman so recently fooled by Harthouse's fey nihilism could be so precise and devastating? Better not to ask. Dickens needs this speech for his own didactic purposes, whether or not it is believable. And this brings us to the main problem with Louisa: though she is *Hard Times'* main character, she never really has a life independent of the role she is designed to play in Dickens' *argument*, as opposed to his novel. We find it difficult to become truly interested in her plight, because she has never been truly *interesting* as a character.

## Thomas Gradgrind, Sr

**Key quotes**

'In this life we want nothing but Facts, sir; nothing but Facts!' (p.9)

'He had a particular pride in the phrase eminently practical, which was considered to have a special application to him.' (p.17)

'In gauging fathomless depths with his little mean excise-rod, and in staggering over the universe with his rusty stiff-legged compass, he had meant to do great things.' (p.216)

A successful merchant, Gradgrind has turned his attentions to 'political economy', or what we would now consider part of the study of social policy, and has founded an experimental school. He is living proof that those with good intentions can do the most harm. Insisting that 'facts alone are wanted in life' he has outlawed fancy and imagination, fables and play, art and wonder, at the school and at Stone Lodge. Tom and Louisa are thus condemned to his method every waking moment to catastrophic result. Dickens likens Gradgrind to his namesake, the disciple Thomas, who demanded tangible proof of Jesus' resurrection (p.10). It is not a favourable comparison. A defining characteristic of Gradgrind is his lack of faith. If Gradgrind himself is not categorically evil, his philosophy certainly is. There is more to life than facts and statistics; Gradgrind's reduction of his children's education to these elements renders them mentally and spiritually deformed adults. Young Tom is the worst example of this, though we see the idea more fully treated in Louisa.

Indeed, good and evil can seem to struggle for ascendancy in each of Gradgrind's actions. (Dickens tells us that he might have been a very kind man indeed (p.32), if it weren't for his slavish adherence to statistics.) This contradiction is well illustrated by his treatment of Sissy: if it is a kindness to take her on at Stone Lodge, it is a cruelty to set as a condition that she never refer to her past (or even think of it). He sees Sissy less as a person than as an opportunity to prove his method.

## Key point

Here we realise that the greatest failing of the adherents of Gradgrind's world view is their lack of humanity, especially when they think of themselves as acting in the service of humanity.

Again, Gradgrind is not evil by intention; his lack of humanity results from his lack of imagination. Gradgrind is simply incapable of understanding that the 'teeming myriads of human beings around him' (p.95) consist of more than the statistics that can be kept on their behaviour.

Over the course of the novel Gradgrind undergoes a change, coming to realise, with Louisa's breakdown, that his system is bankrupt. Where he had previously seemed a dynamo, he is now cautious, unsure of himself and unprecedentedly at a loss for words. We might conclude that he had been fairly weak all along, and that he has merely gone from the orbit of one strong character to that of another, namely from Bounderby to Sissy. The pugnacious Gradgrind, the inhuman Gradgrind, the one who would defend the rightness of his system against all evidence, who would use his own children as the subjects for experimentation, is a kind of protégé[12] of the worse Bounderby. The defining moment for this version of Gradgrind is when he advises Louisa to marry his hateful friend based upon the utility of the marriage, rather than on love. But over the years, that other powerful character, Sissy Jupe, pulls him from Bounderby's orbit. After Louisa's bombshell accusation leads him to question the very foundations of his philosophy, Gradgrind essentially puts himself, as well as Louisa, in the care of Sissy (who has been making a happy home at Stone Lodge for his other children). It turns out that Gradgrind himself was the subject in the experiment that he thought he was performing on Sissy. Her inherent humanity, undamaged by his machinations, ends up providing a model for the better man he becomes.

## Josiah Bounderby

**Key quotes**

'A man who could never sufficiently vaunt himself a self-made man.' (p.20)

'There's no family pride about me, there's no imaginative sentimental humbug about me. I call a spade a spade …' (p.37)

'… that remarkable man and self-made Humbug, Josiah Bounderby of Coketown.' (p.254)

Bounderby is one of the truly memorable characters in *Hard Times*. He is what the Victorians called a 'humbug', a fraud, a phoney and a braggart, who spouts his cock-and-bull story about the disadvantages of his youth at every opportunity. When it is unveiled as a lie late in the novel, Bounderby moves in our eyes from being merely detestable to downright

12 A *protégé* of a person is someone under their friendly protection and influence.

bizarre. Why, one asks, did he find it necessary to concoct such a tale in the first place? What need does it fulfil?

While other men of his class (capitalists who have amassed the kind of wealth to which only landed nobility could previously have claimed) are playing down their origins and buying themselves titles, Bounderby does the opposite – he invents for himself an origin far below the one he knew. It can only be because he wants to make his achievement seem greater than it is, greater than the other robber barons of Coketown. Bounderby uses the lowly origins he claims as justification to make pronouncements on other people's behaviour or position.

Yet there is a viciousness to Bounderby that cannot be so easily explained. Note how he truly relishes the fall of Nickits from a position of success similar to his (Book 2, Chapter 7), and how he forces Mrs Sparsit to revisit and even embellish her privileged origin, so as to take maximal satisfaction in her current position as his housekeeper. He advises Gradgrind to kick Sissy out of the school, unmoved that her father has left her. He accuses any worker who complains about the terrible working conditions in his factory, or any other matter, of having aspirations to 'turtle soup and venison' (p.126). He even accuses Louisa of such ambitions when their marriage fails, though she has shown no interest in his wealth.

But the most important thing about Bounderby is his secret. Far from having a terrible childhood and a mother who deserted him, he was the product of a supportive, sacrificing family. He has been paying his mother a pittance wage under the condition that she never come to Coketown. This is the cruellest of Bounderby's many cruelties. Remember that as a bachelor, he has been supporting Mrs Sparsit as his housekeeper – a job that his widowed mother, alone and suffering ill health, could be occupying.

### Key point

In Bounderby, Dickens is telling us something about the dangers of making myths about oneself. Like many people who have 'made it', Bounderby has created a myth to make his achievement seem greater than it is. Though he pretends not to care about class and standing, the fact that he is so ashamed of his mother reveals him to be painfully class conscious, just another striving man – one of the 'turtle soup' brigade.

A person who has elevated himself from the lowest position owes no consideration to anyone, and so Bounderby's myth allows him to give free reign to his inherent cruelty. In the bigger picture, Dickens might be telling us that super-capitalism depends on just such cruelty, and that those who partake in it must create a myth of one kind or another in order to justify that cruelty.

## Stephen Blackpool

### Key quotes

'He had known, to use his words, a peck of trouble.' (p.66)

'He was a good power-loom weaver, and a man of perfect integrity.' (p.66)

'Now, a' God's name … show me the law to help me!' (p.76)

'He had been for many years a quiet silent man, associating but little with other men …' (p.143)

'It was even harder than he could have believed possible to separate in his own conscience his abandonment by all his fellows, from a baseless sense of shame and disgrace.' (p.143)

'A muddle! Aw a muddle!' (p.263)

Stephen Blackpool is a magnet for disaster. At an early age he married a woman who turned out to be a hopeless and dangerous drunk. She occasionally returns to Coketown to hock some furniture and make his life miserable before disappearing once again. The worst of all this is that Stephen has been in love with Rachael for years, a relationship that has had to remain platonic because of this matrimonial entanglement. There is no recourse; divorce from his wife would require an Act of Parliament, out of the question for a poor weaver.

Then there is the trouble he finds at work. Because of a promise he seems to have made to Rachael (Dickens has forgotten to tell us what it is), Stephen refuses to join the union that is forming at Bounderby's factory. He is vilified[13] for this decision by the troublemaker Slackbridge and ostracised[14] at the factory. Yet Stephen defends the unionists to Bounderby, telling him why there is such discontent in the slave camp he calls a factory. After Bounderby fires him (knowing that no one else will ever hire a man dismissed under such circumstances), Louisa puts it best, saying that he is 'sacrificed alike' by the 'prejudices' of both classes in Coketown, workers and owners (p.156). Before he can leave Coketown and Rachael forever, one more insult awaits Stephen Blackpool; young Tom Gradgrind contrives to set him up as the fall guy for the robbery he is planning at the bank.

Little wonder that Stephen refers to his life as a 'muddle' that nothing will remedy but death – and this remedy comes in the form of a fall down an abandoned mine shaft. Stephen is drawn as a man of perfect integrity and forbearance. One can't help feeling he would have been a more interesting character if he had been given a little less of each. Dickens aims for stirring pathos in the scenes between Rachael and Stephen, but they are the flattest things in the novel. The problem stems from the fact that Stephen, made to bear the load of so many of the injustices that Dickens wants to address (inequitable divorce laws, hideous working conditions in factories, unscrupulous union activities, the absolute power wielded by factory owners), is less a character than a vehicle for discussion. There is some fine, experimental writing on display when Dickens writes from the inside of his mind, most notably the brilliant dream in which Stephen poisons his wife and is hanged for it (Book 1, Chapter 13), but this eternal victim is never given a chance to be much else.

---

13 *To vilify* someone means to speak evil of them or to defame them.

14 *To ostracise* someone means to completely exclude them from a group.

## James Harthouse

### Key quotes

'I assure you I attach not the least importance to any opinions. ... any set of ideas will do just as much good as any other set ...' (p.129)

'The only difference between us and the professors of virtue or benevolence, or philanthropy ... is, that we know it is all meaningless, and say so ...' (p.162)

'... it were much better for the age in which he lived, that he and the legion of whom he was one were designedly bad, than indifferent and purposeless.' (p.175)

Harthouse is the model of the perfect London gentleman – he is handsome, elegant, eloquent, pampered, precious and bored. He has been everywhere, and found nothing to interest him. Not because nothing is interesting, but because it is fashionable not to be interested in anything, and Harthouse lacks the imagination to scorn fashion. Needing a career of some kind, he is convinced to 'go in' for Gradgrind and his 'facts men', but he never pretends to believe in the Gradgrind system. Indeed, he makes a virtue of not believing in anything. Taken by Louisa's beauty, he sets out to seduce her in his unfocused way and nearly succeeds – not because of his considerable charm, but because of his staged nihilism. Louisa has come to the conclusion that 'nothing matters' as a kind of defence mechanism against the sterility of her upbringing; hence she takes comfort in Harthouse's disgusting assertion that 'virtue, benevolence and philanthropy' are 'meaningless' (p.162).

### Key point

Dickens repeatedly refers to Harthouse as a demon or even as the devil himself, suggesting that people who do not believe in anything are more dangerous than those who start out with evil intentions.

Dickens takes some pains to draw parallels between Harthouse's moral lassitude and Gradgrind's energetic wrong-headedness. Both pursue the ideal 'never wonder', Gradgrind from a perverted view of the usefulness of facts, Harthouse from pure laziness. Not even the opium he seems to smoke in that pipe of his can induce any wonder in him.

Harthouse habitually uses his charms to manipulate people, once their defences have been undermined, but he finds himself no match for Sissy Jupe. In the same way that Stephen Blackpool, a man with no real-world 'power', is the only one in the novel to stand up to Bounderby, Sissy, the 'abandoned stroller's daughter' is alone in seeing how powerless Harthouse really is, despite his credentials. In both cases, Dickens wants us to see that the greatest authority (if, alas, not the only one) is moral authority; to defeat his 'devil', Dickens sends against him the character most imbued with the 'virtue, benevolence and philanthropy' he ridicules.

## Thomas Gradgrind, Jr ('the whelp')

### Key quotes

'I am sick of my life, Loo. I hate it altogether, and I hate everybody except you.' (p.54)

'It was altogether unaccountable that a young gentleman whose imagination had been strangled in the cradle, should still be inconvenienced by its ghost in the form of grovelling sensualities; but such a monster, beyond all doubt, was Tom.' (p.132)

Raised in the same manner as Louisa, Tom shows a rather different way of dealing with his upbringing. From the start, there is a violence in him; where Louisa stares at her fire, convincing herself of the meaningless of life, Tom, likening himself to a donkey who wants to kick, aspires to revenge (pp.54–5). As Tom becomes an adult, the desire for revenge is diluted by aimless and self-destructive 'pursuits', such as gambling and other unnamed vices. Dickens, whose ability to achieve the perfect phrase can be startling, calls him a 'monster of grovelling sensualities' (p.132). Denied a childhood, Tom ends up weak and snivelling, hating the world, childlike, in the worst ways that term implies. Louisa loves him, but he takes advantage of this sole bounty to convince her to marry Bounderby (to make his life at the latter's bank a little easier), and after, immune to her misery, he plies her with demands for money. On the night of the robbery she begs him to tell the truth about it, but Tom turns to the wall (Book 2, Chapter 8). He is finished; from this point in the novel, he will come to hate his sister openly, will become a fugitive, will even lash out at those who save him from just punishment for the crime.

## Mrs Sparsit

**Key quotes**

'... she had a self-laudatory sense of correcting, by her ladylike deportment, the rude business aspect of the place.' (p.113)

'It soon appeared that if Mrs Sparsit had a failing ... it was that she was so excessively regardless of herself and regardful of others, as to be a nuisance.' (p.181)

Another wholly negative character, Mrs Sparsit is also a lot of fun. Dickens concocts some of his most delicious writing about the sordid pedigree of this 'high-born lady' (Mrs Scadgers and her mysterious leg; Mr Sparsit and his death by brandy, pp.46–7). Though of a different nature, her pretensions to humility are a match even for Bounderby's. To his street-urchin-turned-fat-cat, Mrs Sparsit plays aristocrat laid low by circumstance. It is part of Bounderby's peculiar psychology that he *needs* Mrs Sparsit to act this part. His constant reminders of her origin (and present position) are obviously meant to set his elevation in even bolder relief.

Yet Bounderby is truly in awe of this woman; she is the only one whose opinion he fears. Even today in England (and elsewhere) the fawning of the merely rich over those with titles before their names (no matter how mortgaged their estate or nauseous their personality) is not quite extinct. Mrs Sparsit's deference to Bounderby is of course a sham, undertaken to maintain her position. When he marries Louisa, she goes into full attack mode, undermining Bounderby's opinion of his new wife at every opportunity. Has Mrs Sparsit 'set her cap' for Bounderby as Tom implies? (p.136). It's certainly possible; remember, the deceased Mr Sparsit was

15 years her junior – this seems about the difference in age between her and Bounderby. But she needn't have such designs in order to want to see Louisa's fall, and her consequent restoration to her former position. She pursues this goal implacably to her eventual doom.

## Sissy Jupe

**Key quotes**

(Of her father) 'I keep the nine oils ready for him, and I know he will come back.' (p.64)

'... the once deserted girl shone like a beautiful light upon the darkness of [Louisa].' (p.220)

Sissy is one of the entirely positive figures in *Hard Times*. A ministering angel to more than one character, her essential feature is fidelity. She is the comfort and moral support of her father, remaining loyal to him after he abandons her and the circus. It is important that Sissy accepts Gradgrind's proposal to look after her only because it is what her father would have wanted. Though miserable at Stone Lodge and the school, she remains there out of loyalty to those wishes. Dickens wants us to understand that these qualities are the foundation upon which she is able to achieve her considerable good deeds. She performs good deeds throughout the novel: she introduces tenderness and love to Stone Lodge, she rehabilitates Louisa after the latter's breakdown and guides her to a moral world view, dispatches the diabolical Harthouse from Coketown, she takes an active role in trying to clear Stephen Blackpool and later she tries to prevent young Tom's arrest. Sissy is of course a failure at Gradgrind's school, and this is the best demonstration of its noxious effect (among the school's 'successful' pupils are the shattered Louisa, the amoral Tom and the scheming Bitzer).

## Minor characters

**Rachael** is Stephen Blackpool's true love. They cannot marry, because he is already married, and in order to protect Rachael's reputation, Stephen even limits his contact with her. Perhaps even more forbearing and loyal than Stephen, Rachael is quite a bit too good to be true. **Bitzer** is a model student at Gradgrind's school as a child, and a model of the self-centred, amoral political economy Gradgrind's philosophy champions. The way Bitzer has condemned his mother to the workhouse parallels Bounderby's treatment to his mother. **Sleary** is the man who runs the circus, where Sissy's father was a clown. He plays an important role in the escape of Tom, but more importantly serves as a corrective to Gradgrind and his utilitarian philosophy, insisting that people need recreation and entertainment to ease their labour. His is a rough hewn voice for humanity and the mysterious power of love. **Slackbridge** is the opposite, an obnoxious voice speaking out in a good cause. An agitator for labour reform from outside Coketown, Slackbridge is a manipulator of people's opinions and a brimstone orator.[15] He compares Stephen, who won't join the union, to Judas Iscariot[16] and instigates his being 'sent to Coventry'.

---

15 *Brimstone* is sulphur, the fuel of hell-fire. *Oratory* is the art of giving speeches. So a *brimstone orator* is a speech-maker who tries to inspire the fear of hell in his or her listeners.

16 Judas Iscariot was the disciple who betrayed Jesus.

# THEMES, IDEAS & VALUES

## Themes

### The effects of industrialisation

Dickens reveals the problems associated with rapid industrialisation in his depiction of Coketown and its inhabitants. One of Dickens' greatest gifts was the ability to create vivid settings; in Coketown he exceeds himself. Devoid of any of the benefits bestowed by industrialism upon England's great manufacturing cities – the museums, libraries, parks, cultural centres – Coketown displays all the evils of modernity that Dickens discerned. It is a place where '[n]ature was as strongly bricked out as the killing airs and gases were bricked in' (p.65). It is a labyrinth, overcrowded and stunted, thrust together piecemeal to accommodate the ever growing masses of 'hands' coming in from the country. Its waterways run black and purple with the chemical effluents of manufacture. Its atmosphere is so choked with smoke that the sun is all but obscured, creating a uniform gloom no matter what the season. In other words, it is a place totally unnatural where the things of the natural world have either been 'bricked out' or so distorted as to make something entirely different, a kind of dark parody of nature. We feel this in the bizarre imagery Dickens employs, the 'serpents of smoke' drifting around the factories, the pistons of the machinery going up and down like the 'head of an elephant in a state of melancholy madness' (p.27). Nature is being mocked by the industrialists of Coketown, it is being contained, poisoned, deformed until it no longer resembles anything with which we are familiar.

And if it is a kind of mutation, it houses a mutated social polity, one with vicious social conventions – new laws for a new jungle. In Coketown the pursuit of profit requires the suppression of traditional social values (the protection of the weak, Christian charity, the importance of human warmth, etc.). Gradgrind's unholy philosophy is used to fill the gap created by their loss. It asserts that self-interest should be the mover of all social interaction, that a person's value depends entirely on her utility, that statistics will cure human woes and that wonder is dangerous to humanity. The buildings in Coketown all look the same, which is mirrored by the fact that its workers, now regarded as machines, have lost their individuality. Reformers wring their hands because no one attends its many churches, not admitting that religion too has been replaced by the construction of new idols. Again and again Dickens employs biblical allusions with the purpose of demonstrating how far the prevailing philosophies and practices in Coketown have strayed from the Christianity that was such a major part of Victorian life.[17] Its factories are altars for a new religion of consumption and profit; their smokestacks are new towers of Babel (p.81). (See p.312 of the text, Ch.12, n.4, for a note on the tower of Babel.)

Coketown is really a classic dystopia, an invention worthy of Orwell.[18] The difference is that Dickens was delineating a reality (perhaps even worse than he evokes) that was being lived, rather than one looming on the horizon. Coketown may be an invention, but Dickens' description of it was based in reality.

## Home

If we think of Coketown as the 'home' of the novel, we will see that it is the model for all the other homes portrayed in *Hard Times*, namely the Gradgrind residence (Stone Lodge), Bounderby's country estate and Stephen Blackpool's room. Rather than 'homes', these are merely places, places of dislocation or isolation, of disaffection and conflict. Stone Lodge is the most interesting case. Aptly named, containing none of the sympathy or warmth one associates with a home, it is run by the zealous

17 For examples of these see the notes to the Penguin Classics edition of *Hard Times*, edited and with an introduction and notes by Kate Flint (the text referred to in this text guide).

18 A *dystopia* is an imaginary setting where everything is as bad as it possibly can be. George Orwell is famous for his dystopian novel about totalitarianism called *Nineteen Eighty-Four.*

Gradgind just like his school – it is austere, colourless and antiseptic. The family it contains is riven by the elements of dislocation to be found in Coketown. Mrs Gradgrind is an even worse offender against traditional family than her husband; he is merely wrongheaded, but she is distant and ineffectual. Her children are a nuisance, and even if she could understand the ramifications of the environment her husband has created, there is no reason to assume she would change anything.

Bounderby's country house is possibly worse than Stone Lodge. A luxurious place devoid of love or comfort, it has been taken by Bounderby from the hapless Nickits and retains the character of a usurped kingdom. For Louisa, it serves as a second prison to replace Stone Lodge.

Stephen Blackpool's lodgings are sparse and unwelcoming, a reflection of his social station, but it is the threat that hangs over it – the return of his estranged wife – that keeps it from being a home. This is the most extreme case of family dislocation in the novel. Tired after his gruelling workday, Stephen would rather walk the streets than return to his room when his wife is there. For Stephen, as for Louisa, there really is no such thing as home. Louisa at least returns to a changed Stone Lodge in Book 3 to begin a recovery process, but Stephen will find only a series of increasingly inhospitable species of isolation: from his home, from his livelihood, from Coketown, from his beloved Rachael and finally from life itself.

The places that other characters occupy are likewise anything but homes: Mrs Sparsit and Bitzer live for a time in the bank, a place of business, each scheming and plotting their next moves. Similarly, Harthouse occupies a room in a hotel, a symbol of his moral rootlessness. Indeed, the closest thing the novel offers to a home is the one entity that looks least like it, namely Sleary's circus. A group of unrelated people thrown together by their occupation, Sleary's performers truly support each other, also making them the closest thing to a *family* in the novel. In the inhospitable and unnatural domain that is Coketown, the elements we associate with a home – love, warmth and support – can find no foothold. It is somehow fitting that the entity most closely representing these elements is a nomadic circus.

# Ideas

*Hard Times* is a novel of protest, and as such it contains some ideas that would have been controversial in Dickens' time. Much of this guide has been dedicated to unravelling some of the institutions and philosophies Dickens attacks. Here I'd like to focus on some of the solutions or alternatives that he offers. Dickens looks both forwards and backwards in *Hard Times*. The novel calls both for progressive reform and a return to basic values.

### Divorce

Dickens clearly supports reform of the divorce laws of his day. Stephen suffers in his marriage to his wife and seeks advice about a legal separation. By contrast, Bounderby simply discards Louisa and acts as though he was never married to her. Dickens is saying there is a way for the rich and a way for the poor, no matter what the statutes say. Dickens himself separated from his wife, though a few years after the writing of *Hard Times*. Unlike Stephen, he was able to maintain a separate household, and undertake a new relationship. Having no recourse to start again with Rachael, as he would like, Stephen and she must continue to suffer. Dickens wants us to see that the pursuit a new life should not be the exclusive right of the wealthy.

### Work and recreation

Sleary represents his author when he says, 'People mutht be amuthed. They can't be alwayth a learning, nor yet they can't be alwyath a working, they an't made for it' (p.282). This sentiment hardly seems radical to us now, long after the major victories in labour reform have been won. But in Dickens' time it was not unheard of for people to be working 15 hours a day, not because they were ambitious – it was either that or not work at all. Such work was done by children too, even after measures restricting child labour were enacted. Reform is always slow and often timid; it cannot gain momentum until there is sufficient public opinion to support it.

In *Hard Times* we witness a kind of debate about the issue: on one side there is the delusional Bounderby and on the other is the reality of characters like Rachael and Stephen. Again, Bounderby is not a mere buffoon. His cock-and-bull story about the degradation of his upbringing gives him an excuse to show no sympathy to his workers, to drive them mercilessly and discard them when they stumble, to berate them as shiftless and mercenary (after all, weren't his circumstances much worse?). Stephen does not attempt to offer a solution to the labour crisis that is brewing in his speech at Bounderby's house (Book 2, Chapter 5), though he does give his opinion about what methods must be pursued. There must be patience, compromise, the ability by those in power to see the workers' side and not just the manufacturers'. Above all there must be a willingness to see the workers as humans rather than as 'figures in a [sum] or machines' (p.149). The Bounderbys of the world considered any burden placed upon labourers acceptable as long as there remained a large pool from which to draw. They had all the power in the *Hard Times* years. Dickens underscores this truth when Bounderby dismisses Stephen from his livelihood for his remarks. He is outargued, but he imposes his will nevertheless. In the novel's debate our sympathies obviously go out to the Rachaels and Stephens and away from the Bounderbys. Eventually public opinion followed suit.

But it is frightening to think that there should have been a debate at all. And, sadly, this is not ancient history after all. In parts of the world people are facing the same dilemmas Stephen and Rachael face – crushing workloads, grinding poverty or perhaps both. Globalisation is the new reality, and whether it has done more to create such situations or relieve them is a question I will not attempt to answer. But unquestionably we are awakening to the fact that our economic activities can have a profound impact on the lives of people far away. Globalisation has also had an impact in the West, because as competition for cheap labour has gone international, working conditions in the 'first world' have changed. Some of the rock-solid reforms won in the past – concerning pensions for example – have become unnervingly susceptible to erosion. And it is not just the Bounderbys of today who are willing to accept the resurgence of a class with which Dickens was familiar, the so-called working poor.[19]

On the other side of the coin, the legal working week (between 36 and 40 hours in most industrialised countries) is something of a joke for many of the professions. Ask a young investment banker or lawyer when he or she last worked so 'short' a week. The salaries that such jobs garner are indisputably attractive, yet the requirements for keeping them are becoming more and more Dickensian. Our age has given this subject its own rubric – 'life/work balance' – itself a testament to the fact that Sleary's statement is still pertinent and the debate has not ended.

## The dangers of utilitarianism

Dickens is espousing the idea that to look merely at the utilitarian value of anything – a person or a resource, the land itself or the roles that individuals have to play in a society – cannot but result in a poisoned atmosphere, quite literally in the case of Coketown. The worst offenders in *Hard Times*, Gradgrind and Bounderby, dismiss the traditional roles played by morality and imagination to create a new calculus by which to judge the value of human beings. This utilitarianism is the foundation upon which Coketown is built, and it is the philosophy that pollutes the air. Human relationships, too, are poisoned, even between positive characters, who have to overcome some crippling aspect of the value that governing social bodies have ascribed to them. Though Sissy is unfathomably morally superior to Gradgind, he sees her as the incorrigible 'stroller's child', and it is his label that sticks.

Stephen, a man of perfect integrity, is smeared by the utterly contemptible Slackbridge, the revolutionary. He is also condemned by Bounderby, who as a factory owner is a member of the *bourgeoisie*. Bounderby and Slackbridge, who are otherwise mortal enemies, behave in the same despicable way towards Stephen, and he is powerless to

19 In the United States, for example, a full-time worker at Wal-Mart, one of the world's largest and richest companies, earns a salary that puts him or her below the poverty line.

do anything about it. Now, such inequities don't need the excuse of utilitarianism to flourish, but that is the governing mentality of Coketown. The divisions between the novel's characters stem from a system of classification that makes a man like Bounderby great and a man like Stephen the lowest of the low.

Dickens clearly saw utilitarianism as a radical philosophy, and, as I have argued, his attacks against it can resemble a genre that had not been identified at the time, the 'futuristic dystopia' (think of *Nineteen Eighty-Four*, *Brave New World* or even *Blade Runner*). The solution he espouses to such thinking might well have been called reactionary even in his time. It includes a return to the 'Christian' values of charity and compassion, a return to a way of life where people had more leisure, more room to live and better air to breathe and a return to a sense of community that he sees as being eroded by the requirements of the industrialised economy. In other words, there is a longing in *Hard Times*, more implied than declared, for a return to a pre-industrialised England.

### The importance of childhood

The lives of Louisa and Tom are spoiled because Gradgrind deprives them of their childhood. Just as recreation is important to adult workers, imagination, play and fancy (and the time to indulge them) are essential to the wellbeing of children. This seems more than basic to us now, but it was not so in Dickens' day. Nor is it in many parts of the world 150 years later. It is estimated that 250 million children around the world work, often under conditions as bad as those Dickens describes. We should not forget another child in *Hard Times*, mentioned only in passing. Rachael's sister, who died 'young and misshapen' (p.263), her health destroyed by the conditions of Coketown – one assumes from working in the factories. She is there to remind us that it is not just misguided thinking that steals childhoods, but poverty and the greed that sends children to work and not to school. Dickens assures us that no less than the health of a society depends on how well it treats its children.

## Values

Almost without exception, the main characters in *Hard Times* can be classified into one of two groups: the wholly positive or the wholly negative. The first group includes the sainted Rachael and Sissy and the long suffering Stephen; the second contains Bounderby, Harthouse, Mrs Sparsit and young Tom Gradgrind. Even minor characters fall neatly into these camps: Sleary and Mrs Pegler in the former, Slackbridge and Bitzer in the latter. There are complications: Gradgrind Sr begins firmly in the negative group, remaining there for the first two-thirds of the novel before migrating to the positive. The only character to occupy anything like a grey area is Louisa. This should not be a surprise: *Hard Times'* main plot hinges on her seduction by Harthouse and her consequent reclamation to the good by Sissy. Dickens realised that he needed to present clear distinctions between the morality of his characters for the battle for Louisa to have its impact. *Hard Times* is much more a morality tale than it is a study in psychology, and as Dickens navigates Louisa between the rocks, he also highlights what he considers to be the great moral questions of his time. By examining the values of his characters we can get a better understanding of Dickens' message.

## Values critiqued by the text

### Self-interest

*Hard Times'* negative characters are above all self-serving. Bounderby, Tom, Harthouse and Mrs Sparsit are willing to dispense with all traditional morality in the pursuit of their desires. Tom's case is a bit easier to understand than Bounderby's. Denied any moral guardianship in his youth, Tom turns out to be a slave to 'grovelling sensualities' as a man. Needing money, he steals from Bounderby's bank, framing an innocent man and destroying him in the process. Yet few readers would blame Tom entirely; he is the product of his father's system. His nickname, 'the whelp', is very appropriate. *Whelp* is a word for the young of a variety of animals, but can also be used as a derogatory term for an immature youth. Tom's is a case of arrested development. In him, the self-centredness of early childhood has become monstrous in the manhood for which he has not been prepared.

Bounderby, on the other hand, is a slave to his self-image. Having concocted a story of degradation and disadvantage, he uses it as an excuse to behave in an utterly selfish manner. His outrageous fake humility is comical, but Bounderby can also be vicious. He takes a part equal to Tom's in ruining Stephen's life, basically on a whim. Yet Bounderby's worst sin is committed against his mother, Mrs Pegler, whom he forces to live alone on a pittance so that he can preserve his image of himself. Her health fails during the novel, underscoring just how cruel Bounderby's strategy is. The place she should be occupying in his home is given to the malicious Mrs Sparsit. Bounderby and Tom share the quality of total ingratitude to family members who have supported them, Bounderby to his mother and Tom to his sister Louisa. In the moral universe of *Hard Times* there can be no worse sin than this.

### Gradgrind's philosophy

The worst of the values that Dickens attacks are those held by Gradgrind for most of the novel. Gradgrind teaches his students that the world can be explained, and indeed improved, by the study of fact to the exclusion of anything having to do with the imagination or traditional morality. It is important to remember that Gradgrind is a committed reformer, not a mere dabbler in educational methods, and he has replaced the traditional values of reform – empathy, justice and charity – with statistics and calculation. Harthouse refers to him as a machine (p.226), and he is not far wrong. Gradgrind is the perfect figure of a man who has lost his humanity to the mechanical age, a prophet of the thinking that has been derived from the revolutionary mechanical successes of the 'modern' era (that is, Dickens' mid-nineteenth century).

Gradgrind truly believes that one can *fix* the lives of countless people by approaching those lives as if they were parts in one great machine. The tools to be used are statistics and empirical 'fact'. The influences to be outlawed (think of them as the grime and dust that might break down the machinery) are fancy, wonder, imagination. As Dickens writes, Gradgrind has 'no need to cast an eye on the teeming myriad of human beings around him, but could settle all their destinies on a slate, and wipe out all their tears with one dirty little bit of sponge' (p.95). A reformer who knows nothing about humans, yet believes that all their troubles can be solved by dry calculation is indeed a kind of machine; worse, he is very dangerous to anyone who might come under his power. The novel shows us the devastating effect Gradgrind's mechanistic method has on Tom and Louisa. They have been denied so much of what it means to be human in their education and they grow into depraved and damaged humans.

Many of the other negative characters in the novel exemplify another of Gradgrind's doctrines, that a person's actions in the social sphere should be motivated exclusively by self-interest. We have already discussed to what degree this is true in Bounderby and Tom. Gradgrind really sees the effects of his teaching when Bitzer arrives at the circus to return Tom to Coketown. Bitzer shows no malice towards Tom, but is merely following the principles that have been drummed into his head.

Though the selfless actions of Rachael and Sissy refute Gradgrind's doctrines better than any words could, Dickens uses Sleary as the mouthpiece for his views. He tells Gradgrind that 'there ith a love in the world, not all Thelf-interest after all', and that this love 'hath a way of ith own of calculating or not calculating' (p.282). Further, this love is very difficult to define precisely. One recalls Hamlet's advice to Horatio, that there are more things on heaven and earth than are dreamed of in Horatio's philosophy. Dickens asserts again and again that Gradgrind's dismaying suppositions about humanity are due more than anything else to a lack of imagination. Reductive philosophies like Gradgrind's utilitarianism will never supply answers to human woes, because they take as their starting point a supposition that people can be easily understood. Like Shakespeare, Dickens teaches us that humans are complicated, mercurial and that their behaviour can be very difficult to predict.

## Values endorsed by the text

### Charity and self-sacrifice

Sissy's self-sacrifice is contrasted with the self-centredness of Bounderby and Tom. Like Rachael, Sissy is entirely altruistic. Whether reading to her disconsolate father, raising Gradgrind's children or intervening to save Louisa from Harthouse, her every action in the novel is performed to improve someone else's lot. This is the essence of what Dickens would have called Christian charity (a generosity of spirit over which no religion can claim ownership). This is the opposite of Bounderby's selfishness, or Harthouse's, or Tom's, etc. It is interesting that this altruism is only practised by the novel's least powerful characters, namely Sissy and Rachael, yet it is presented by Dickens as a power unto itself.

### Loyalty

Loyalty is another quality practised by the positive characters in *Hard Times*. Sissy hangs onto the bottle of nine oils, a talisman of her loyalty to her father; Rachael remains loyal to Stephen, even though they cannot marry (we should not dismiss the considerable financial consequences of Rachael's decision not to marry someone else), and she fights to clear his name later. Contrast the loyalty practised in Sleary's circus to that found in Bounderby's factory, where he dismisses his 'hands' outright as lazy and scheming, and they organise to protect themselves against him (in the process ostracising Stephen, one of their own). Harthouse's 'going in for' the 'fact men' without even pretending to believe in their mission is also opposite to the loyalty practised at Sleary's. It is not hard to find other examples: Mrs Sparsit's scheming to undermine her employer's happiness and Tom's stealing from the bank. There is an interesting moment towards the end of the novel when Gradgrind Senior tries to get Bitzer to relent in his pursuit of Tom by appealing to any sense of loyalty Bitzer might feel towards him. But Bitzer has learned Gradgrind's method all to well: his education was a contract, derived from self-interest on both sides, and loyalty has nothing to do with it. 'Gratitude was to be abolished, and the virtues springing from it were not to be' (p.278).

## How Dickens emphasises his values

Dickens clearly emphasises the values that he endorses by showing us the consequences of each characters' actions. The positive characters in *Hard Times* behave utterly correctly – as though to behave immorally would be constitutionally impossible. Each of the negative characters eventually suffers, either with the burden of guilt (Tom), or shame (Harthouse), or by being ensnared in the traps they have laid for others (Mrs Sparsit), or in the revelation of the elaborate hoaxes they have perpetrated (Bounderby). The book's worst punishment is paradoxically reserved for its best character, Stephen, who first sees his reputation ruined and then dies a miserable death attempting to clear his name. But Dickens was a reformer, and Stephen is a sacrifice to the cause.

Without question, the author is unambiguous about what constitutes right behaviour, and he demonstrates it for us by contrasting the values of his characters. Against Gradgrind's utilitarianism is Sissy's humanity; against Bounderby's self-serving is Rachael's charity; against Slackbridge's manipulation is Stephen's integrity; against Mrs Sparsit's scheming is Sissy's support; against Tom's dishonesty is Stephen's honesty; against Bounderby's betrayal of his mother is Sissy's loyalty to her father; against Harthouse's nihilism is Rachael's faith; and against Gradgrind's bankrupt philosophy is Sleary's generous world view.

# DIFFERENT INTERPRETATIONS

*Hard Times* is anything but ambiguous. Creative reading is always to be encouraged, but it is pretty clear what Dickens thinks about the world of Coketown and its inhabitants. Still, any text can benefit from taking multiple perspectives on it. At the same time that *Hard Times* is a meditation on the importance of childhood, it is also an exposé on labour relations and industrial practice. At the same time that it is a tale of doomed romance (between Stephen and Rachael), it is an early investigation of class struggle. It is a kind of *Bildungsroman*[20] about a Victorian woman (Louisa) at the same time that it is a treatise against the crimes of utilitarianism and in favour of the values of charity, loyalty and tolerance. These are all different aspects of the book that cannot really be understood as a whole if any of them are overlooked.

## Towards a Marxist reading

One interesting perspective that could be developed further is a Marxist reading. At the time Charles Dickens was serialising *Hard Times* in London, Karl Marx was living in the same city, in very dire straits, but active in the international labour and communist movements that would become synonymous with his name. Friedrich Engels, Marx's writing partner and financial supporter, was living in Manchester, working at a cotton mill owned, in part, by his father. Though neither was English, much of their thought on class struggle, historical materialism, the economics of capital, private property, etc. was developed out of their observations of English capitalism. In Engels' case, his observations came directly from the very environment of *Hard Times*. Indeed, Slackbridge, the unionist rabblerouser, drawn as such a villain by Dickens, is a man very much of Marx's ilk, educated, intellectual, eloquent and most

20 *Bildungsroman* is German for 'novel of development' and describes novels that show the development of a character from childhood and immaturity to adulthood.

importantly, an outsider, intent on bringing a universalist solution to Coketown's problems. Of course Slackbridge's discourse (way of talking), peppered with biblical allusions, is not much like Marx's, who was an atheist and did not particularly relish public-speaking or large groups.

Marx's basic idea about class struggle came from an overall view of history as 'dialectical'. He believed that major historical transformation only comes about from the struggle between opposing elements and that the result of this clash is an entirely new reality. Looked at in economic terms, Marx contended that the realities of capitalist production would always create a struggle between those who ran the means of production, and those who did the work. The pursuit of capital creates diminishing returns, so those who laboured would never be able to share in the profits created by manufacture. Thus they would become alienated from the process, adrift and treated as a commodity. So far this sounds relevant to Dickens' perspective on the labour crisis. Marx and Engels were, like Dickens, great sympathisers with working people, Engels publishing an exposé on the conditions of workers in England as early as 1845. Indeed, 'alienation' is probably the single best word to describe Stephen Blackpool's plight throughout the course of *Hard Times*. The antagonism between the union at Bounderby's mill and Bounderby himself would be described by Marx as the class antagonism that cannot help but erupt from capitalistic production; it is as inevitable as the item being produced. Marx holds that manufactured goods, become 'fetishes', unnatural and oppressive elements both to the labourers, who take part in making them (but cannot afford to buy them), and the capitalists who become enslaved, in a way, to maintaining their lifestyles. This idea also seems germane to Dickens' drawing of the capitalist Bounderby, always disparaging the fineries with which he surrounds himself, and the impoverished circumstances of Stephen and Rachael.

Marx contended that humans only fulfilled their own potential, in other words became truly human, by providing an existence for themselves out of a hostile natural environment. But when individual or community sustenance gives way to mass production, that essential human element is removed. Labourers are not taking part in full sustenance; they are merely providing one of many functions. Paradoxically (because he had said that humans must overcome nature), people find themselves in a very unnatural position. The result is further alienation, further antagonism between the ones who control production and those who provide individual labour. This unnatural environment is perfectly characterised by Coketown.

In many ways Dickens and Marx and Engels were pulling for the same team, but I do not see the author of *Hard Times* as being anything but antagonistic to the pair. In the character of Slackbridge, Dickens seems to be warning about the consequences of the Marxist path. More importantly, Stephen Blackpool's heartfelt discourse to Bounderby about the labour crisis calls for understanding, dialogue, sympathy and negotiation as the only way out of the 'muddle'. Marx was, of course, a revolutionary, who saw the class antagonism he wrote about as leading inevitably to class war and revolution. This would lead to the creation of a new social order, one where the *proletariat* (workers) would be the 'gravediggers' of the *bourgeoisie* (the manufacturers and professions involved with manufacture). This violent dialectic was not something Dickens could have desired, no matter how much he championed England's poor and working classes.

# QUESTIONS & ANSWERS

## Essay topics

1 'Coketown, the setting of *Hard Times*, is as important as any of its characters.'
Do you agree?

2 'Louisa and young Tom were brought up in the same way, yet they act very differently as adults.'
Discuss.

3 'Dickens writes that Gradgrind's character was "not unkind, all things considered".'
Do you agree?

4 'Stephen Blackpool calls his life a "muddle" because he has no control over it.'
Do you agree?

5 '"Never wonder" is a principle shared by Gradgrind and Harthouse, two characters with very different philosophies.'
How do different characters in *Hard Times* display their commitment to this principle?

6 'Gradgrind's assertion that self-interest guides the interactions of human beings is one of the main themes of *Hard Times*.'
Discuss.

7 '*Hard Times* is a protest novel, but the issues it addresses were solved a long time ago.'
Do you agree?

8 'There are no happy homes or supportive families in *Hard Times*.'
Do you agree?

9 '*Hard Times* is about the importance of a person's childhood on his or her later life.'
Discuss.

10 '*Hard Times* is a meditation on class struggle in England in the 1850s.'
Do you agree?

## Analysing a sample topic

**'*Hard Times* is about the importance of a person's childhood on his or her later life.' Discuss.**

- Essay topics generally ask you to look at the entirety of the novel, and so, you should be prepared to consider multiple examples of childhood and resulting adulthood in *Hard Times*, rather than only one. This question asks you to discuss the validity of a proposition – you do not necessarily have to agree with it. Take some time to think about as many as you can of the characters we see both in childhood and adulthood in the novel before taking your position.
- There are three main characters we follow in this way, Louisa, Tom and Sissy, and one minor character, Bitzer. There should be more than enough material to work with in order to answer the question fully. After thinking about the lives of these characters a bit, you are very likely to agree with the statement: it is indeed one of Dickens' intentions to demonstrate the importance of upbringing on the adults we become.
- Begin to formulate your own statement – this is called a thesis statement – to encapsulate the argument you intend to make. As you are going to refer to specific characters in your essay, your thesis statement should be more specific than the statement found in the question. Some further reflection is likely to lead you to realise that there are both positive examples and negative examples in the novel: the disasters that befall Louisa and Tom as adults can be blamed on their education, yet the altruism and faithfulness Sissy displays later were instilled during her upbringing in Sleary's circus. Your thesis statement should allude to this complexity in your argument.
- Now is the time to think seriously about the evidence you will use to support your ideas in the essay. If you know the novel well, you will find yourself with more than enough examples of the ill-effects of Louisa and Tom's childhood, and their consequent problems as adults – likewise with Sissy. While the main thrust of your argument will concern these three, don't forget about Bitzer.

- Pre-writing is as important as writing in constructing a good argument. Set aside ten minutes or so before you start writing the essay itself. On a scrap piece of paper, do some brainstorming: write down your ideas and your examples in a simple list. It is easy to lose track of your evidence while your brain is otherwise occupied in the writing itself. Also make yourself a rough outline once you have worked out what shape your argument is going to take. You can get so caught up in *what* you are saying that you lose track of *how* you were going to say it – and in what order. A simple outline will help enormously; it will allow you to concentrate on making the argument one step at a time, without losing sight of where it is going.
- You are ready to write. Stick to your outline, but don't rule out inspiration. The reality of writing is that once you become focused enough to put words to paper, you are, paradoxically, in a receptive state of mind. You will remember things you forgot you knew. And if a flash of brilliance occurs, use it.
- Only now should you begin your introductory paragraph, because only now do you know where your argument is going. Introductions should do more than merely begin the discussion – they should at least allude to the entire argument.

### Sample introduction

The importance of childhood is one of the main themes of Charles Dickens' *Hard Times*. The terrible problems faced in adulthood by two of its main characters, Louisa and Tom, stem from the misguided education they receive from their father, Mr Gradgrind. Louisa enters a disastrous marriage because she has never been taught to see the value of anything, and Tom becomes a liar and thief. While Tom never recovers, Louisa is helped to a better life by another character, Sissy. Her positive upbringing in Sleary's circus makes her an excellent adult, despite also having to endure a Gradgrind education. Dickens' close examination of the lives of each of these characters demonstrates just how vital a person's childhood is to the adult they become.

# SAMPLE ANSWER

**'Gradgrind's assertion that self-interest guides the interactions of human beings is one of the main themes of *Hard Times*.' Discuss.**

In *Hard Times*, Thomas Gradgrind teaches his students that self-interest is behind all human interactions. Many of the characters in the novel behave in such a way to support his ideas, but they tend to be negative characters, whose plans come to poor or embarrassing ends. On the other hand, some characters act entirely out of altruism. These are the positive characters in *Hard Times*, and though they are not always rewarded, they manage to effect positive change. Dickens definitely takes the idea that people should act out of self-interest as one of his main themes in order to refute it.

The characters who act completely out of self-interest include Mrs Sparsit, Bitzer, Harthouse, Tom and Bounderby. I will look at the last two. Bounderby does nothing that is not in his own self-interest. He is the most self-centred character in the book, and has even created a myth about his upbringing to make his later achievements seem better. He then uses this story to excuse his self-serving, basically claiming that anyone who has had as bad a start as he, is entitled to show no interest in others. The fact that he keeps his mother living apart from him, alone and ill, shows how far he has drifted from basic human kindness. He receives his 'punishment' when Mrs Pegler is revealed to be his mother. His story collapses, and Bounderby goes from being the idol of the rich to a laughing stock.

Tom's story is different. He has had his father's ideas about self-interest drummed into his head until he knows of no other way to act. Through the course of *Hard Times* Tom indulges himself more and more. He induces Louisa to marry Bounderby for his own benefit. He runs up gambling debts, wheedles money from Louisa and eventually robs the bank and blames it on Stephen Blackpool. Tom becomes increasingly miserable, rather than happy. Eventually he hates not only himself, but Louisa, the only person who has ever really loved him. The more he acts out of self-interest, the further he is removed from human company and comfort. This is his 'punishment', just as much as the fact that he has to flee Coketown in shame.

Two characters, Rachael and Sissy, act entirely out of altruism rather than self-interest. Rachael shows the goodness of her character most clearly when she cares for Stephen's drunk wife, who would have died otherwise. This act is made even less self-serving by the fact that if Stephen's wife did die, Rachael and he would be free to marry, the one thing they truly want. Sissy repeatedly does things for others rather than herself. She reads to her father and supports him through his depression; she raises Gradgrind's younger children in a loving manner; and she takes on Louisa's problem with Harthouse and solves it herself. Sissy is 'rewarded' at the end of the novel. She is the only one of the characters who goes on to find true happiness. Rachael loses Stephen, but she lives on to see his name cleared, and she maintains a dignity afterwards that none of the negative characters can achieve.

In *Hard Times*, characters like Bounderby and Tom may have a lot of 'real-world' power. They are able to destroy others and indulge themselves, but in the end they self-destruct because they have only acted out of self-interest. Rachael and Sissy, women with very little 'real-world' power, are able to effect positive change in the novel simply by acting out of altruism rather than self-interest. In the issue raised by Gradgrind's philosophy, it is obvious where Charles Dickens' beliefs lie.

# REFERENCES & READING

## Text

Dickens, Charles 2003, *Hard Times*, ed. Kate Flint, Penguin Classics, London (1854).

## Further reading

Coles, Nicholas 1986, 'The Politics of *Hard Times*: Dickens the Novelist Versus Dickens the Reformer', *Dickens Studies Annual: Essays on Victorian Fiction*, vol. 15.

Friedman, Stanley 1990, 'Sad Stephen and Troubled Louisa: Paired Protagonists in *Hard Times*', *Dickens Quarterly*, vol. 7, no. 2.

Johnson, Patricia 1989, '*Hard Times* and the Structure of Industrialism: The Novel as Factory', *Studies in the Novel*, vol. 21, no. 2.

Samuels, Allen 1992, *Hard Times: An Introduction to the Variety of Criticism*, Macmillan, New York.

Simpson, Margaret 1997, *The Companion to Hard Times*, Greenwood Press, Westport, Connecticut.

Thomas, Deborah 1997, *Hard Times: A Fable of Fragmentation and Wholeness*, Twayne Publishers, New York.

## Websites

Matsuoka, Mitsuharu 2020, *The Dickens Page*, http://victorian-studies.net/Dickens.html